1st Workshop on Multilingual Multimodal Learning (MML 2022)

Dublin, Ireland
27 May 2022

ISBN: 978-1-7138-6747-0

Printed from e-media with permission by:

Curran Associates, Inc.
57 Morehouse Lane
Red Hook, NY 12571

Some format issues inherent in the e-media version may also appear in this print version.

Printed with permission by Curran Associates, Inc. (2023)

Association for Computational Linguistics
209 N. Eighth Street
Stroudsburg, Pennsylvania 18360

Phone: 1-570-476-8006
Fax: 1-570-476-0860

acl@aclweb.org

Additional copies of this publication are available from:

Curran Associates, Inc.
57 Morehouse Lane
Red Hook, NY 12571 USA
Phone: 845-758-0400
Fax: 845-758-2633
Email: curran@proceedings.com
Web: www.proceedings.com

MML 2022

The 1st Workshop on Multilingual Multimodal Learning

Proceedings of the Workshop

May 27, 2022

The MML organizers gratefully acknowledge the support from the following sponsors.

Preface

Welcome to the Workshop on Multilingual Multimodal Learning (MML)! Multilingual multimodal NLP, which presents new and unique challenges. Multilingual multimodal NLP is one of the areas that suffer the most from language imbalance issues. Texts in most multimodal datasets are usually only available in high-resource languages. Further, multilingual multimodal research provides opportunities to investigate culture-related phenomena. On top of the language imbalance issue in text-based corpora and models, the data of additional modalities (e.g. images or videos) are mostly collected from North American and Western European sources (and their worldviews). As a result, multimodal models do not capture our world's multicultural diversity and do not generalise to out-of-distribution data from minority cultures. The interplay of the two issues leads to extremely poor performance of multilingual multimodal systems in real-life scenarios. This workshop offers a forum for sharing research efforts towards more inclusive multimodal technologies and tools to assess them.

This volume includes the 3 papers presented at the workshop. We received a batch of high-quality research papers, and decided to finally accept 3 out of 6 fully reviewed submissions. MML 2022 was co-located with the 60th Annual Meeting of the Association for Computational Linguistics (ACL 2022) and was held on May 27, 2022 as a hybrid workshop.

It is great to see the accepted papers discussing some of the most important topics for MML: evaluating and developing multimodal models for different languages and in low-resource settings.

The first edition of the MML workshop also hosted a shared task on multilingual visually grounded reasoning. The task was centered around the MaRVL dataset. This dataset extends the NLVR2 task to multicultural and multilingual (Indonesian, Mandarin, Swahili, Tamil, Turkish) inputs: Given two images and a textual description, a system needs to predict whether the description applies to both images (True/False). The shared task is developed to encourage new methods for multilingual multimodal models, with the restriction that models should be publicly available or trained on publicly available data to encourage open source.

We take this opportunity to thank the MML program committee for their help and thorough reviews. We also thank the authors who presented their work at MML, and the workshop participants for the valuable feedback and discussions. Finally, we are deeply honored to have four excellent talks from our invited speakers: David Ifeoluwa Adelani, Lisa-Anne Hendricks, Lei Ji, and Preethi Jyothi.

The MML 2022 workshop organizers,

Emanuele Bugliarello, Kai-Wei Chang, Desmond Elliott, Spandana Gella, Aishwarya Kamath, Liunian Harold Li, Fangyu Liu, Jonas Pfeiffer, Edoardo M. Ponti, Krishna Srinivasan, Ivan Vulić, Yinfei Yang, Da Yin

Organizing Committee

Workshop Chairs

Emanuele Bugliarello, University of Copenhagen
Kai-Wei Chang, UCLA
Desmond Elliott, University of Copenhagen
Spandana Gella, Amazon Alexa AI
Aishwarya Kamath, NYU
Liunian Harold Li, UCLA
Fangyu Liu, University of Cambridge
Jonas Pfeiffer, TU Darmstadt
Edoardo Maria Ponti, MILA Montreal
Krishna Srinivasan, Google Research
Ivan Vulić, University of Cambridge & PolyAI
Yinfei Yang, Google Research
Da Yin, UCLA

Invited Speakers

David Ifeoluwa Adelani, Saarland University
Lisa Anne Hendricks, DeepMind
Lei Ji, Microsoft Research Asia
Preethi Jyothi, IIT Bombay

Program Committee

Program Committee

Arjun Reddy Akula, UCLA
Benno Krojer, McGill University
Chen Cecilia Liu, TU Darmstadt
Duygu Ataman, New York University
Constanza Fierro, University of Copenhagen
Gregor Geigle, TU Darmstadt
Hao Tan, Adobe Systems
Kuan-Hao Huang, UCLA
Laura Cabello Piqueras, University of Copenhagen
Rongtian Ye, Aalto University
Rémi Lebret, EPFL
Sebastian Schuster, New York University
Mandy Guo, Cornell University
Zarana Parekh, Carnegie Mellon University

Invited Talk: Multilingual Language Model Adaptive Fine-Tuning: A Study on African Languages

David Ifeoluwa Adelaini
Saarland University

Abstract: Multilingual pre-trained language models (PLMs) have demonstrated impressive performance on several downstream tasks on both high resourced and low-resourced languages. However, there is still a large performance drop for languages unseen during pre-training, especially African languages. One of the most effective approaches to adapt to a new language is language adaptive fine-tuning (LAFT) — fine-tuning a multilingual PLM on monolingual texts of a language using the pre-training objective. However, African languages with large monolingual texts are few, and adapting to each of them individually takes large disk space and limits the cross-lingual transfer abilities of the resulting models because they have been specialized for a single language. As an alternative, we adapt PLM on several languages by performing multilingual adaptive fine-tuning (MAFT) on 17 most-resourced African languages and three other high-resource languages widely spoken on the continent – English, French, and Arabic to encourage cross-lingual transfer learning. Additionally, to further specialize the multilingual PLM, we removed vocabulary tokens from the embedding layer that corresponds to non-African writing scripts before MAFT, thus reducing the model size by 50%. Our evaluation on two multilingual PLMs (AfriBERTa and XLM-R) and three NLP tasks (NER, news topic classification, and sentiment classification) shows that our approach is competitive to applying LAFT on individual languages while requiring significantly less disk space.

Bio: David Ifeoluwa Adelani is a doctoral student in computer science at Saarland University, Saarbrücken, Germany, and an active member of Masakhane NLP - a grassroots organization whose mission is to strengthen and spur NLP research in African languages, for Africans, by Africans. His current research focuses on NLP for African languages, multilingual representation learning, and privacy in NLP.

Invited Talk: Multimodal Video Understanding with Language Guidance

Lei Ji
Microsoft Research Asia

Abstract: Video naturally comprises of multiple modalities including visual content, language (speech text or meta data), as well as audio. Language inside video provides important semantic guidance for multimodal video understanding. On the one hand, language can be taken as side information to enhance video information with fusion mechanism. On the other hand, language can be used as semantic supervision for video representation learning with self-supervised techniques. Multimodal video-language pretraining models trained on a large-scale dataset are effective for multimodal understanding tasks including vision language matching, captioning, sentiment analysis as well multilingual multimodal tasks as a step forward.

Bio: Lei Ji is a senior researcher at the Natural Language Computing group of Microsoft Research Asia. Her research focuses are vision and language multimodal learning, pretraining, and knowledge mining and reasoning. She has published papers at the top-tier conferences including ACL, AAAI, IJCAI, ACMMM, KDD, CIKM, patents, and transferred these innovative techniques to Microsoft products as well as other external partners.

Invited Talk: Digging Deeper into Multimodal Transformers

Lisa Anne Hendricks
DeepMind

Abstract: Multimodal transformers have had great success on a wide variety of multimodal tasks. This talk will consider what factors contribute to their success as well as what still proves challenging for these models. I will first consider how the choice of training dataset, architecture, and loss function contribute to multimodal transformer performance on a zero-shot image retrieval task. Next, using the newly collected SVO-Probes dataset, I will demonstrate that fine-grained verb understanding is challenging for multimodal transformers and offers an interesting testbed to study multimodal understanding.

Bio: Lisa Anne Hendricks is a research scientist on the Language Team at DeepMind. She received her PhD from Berkeley in May 2019, and a BSEE (Bachelor or Science in Electrical Engineering) from Rice University in 2013. Her research focuses on the intersection of language and vision. She is particularly interested in analyzing why models work, explainability, and mitigating/measuring bias in AI models.

Invited Talk: New Challenges in Learning with Multilingual and Multimodal Data

Preethi Jyothi
IIT Bombay

Abstract: During communication, humans can naturally combine their knowledge about different languages and process simultaneous cues from different modalities. Even as machine learning has made great strides in natural language processing, problems related to multilinguality and multimodality remain largely unsolved. In recent years, each of these issues has received significant attention from the research community. In this talk, we will discuss some of our work on both multilinguality and multimodality, specifically code-switching and audio-visual learning, respectively. Further, towards understanding the additional difficulties that arise when multilinguality and multimodality are present together, we will also describe our recent work on a new multimodal multilingual dataset in Indian languages.

Bio: Preethi Jyothi is an Assistant Professor in the Department of Computer Science and Engineering at IIT Bombay. Her research interests are broadly in machine learning applied to speech and language, specifically focusing on Indian languages and low-resource settings. She was a Beckman Postdoctoral Fellow at the University of Illinois at Urbana-Champaign from 2013 to 2016. She received her Ph.D. from The Ohio State University in 2013. Her doctoral thesis dealt with statistical models of pronunciation in conversational speech and her work on this topic received a Best Student Paper award at Interspeech 2012. She co-organised a research project on probabilistic transcriptions at the 2015 Jelinek Summer Workshop on Speech and Language Technology, for which her team received a Speech and Language Processing Student Paper Award at ICASSP 2016. She was awarded a Google Faculty Research Award in 2017 for research on accented speech recognition. She currently serves on the ISCA SIGML board and is a member of the Editorial Board of Computer Speech and Language.

Table of Contents

Program

Friday, May 27, 2022

09:20 - 09:30	*Opening Remarks*
09:30 - 10:30	*Invited Talk 1: David Ifeoluwa Adelaini*
10:30 - 11:00	*Coffee Break*
11:00 - 12:00	*Invited Talk 2: Lei Ji*
12:00 - 12:30	*Findings from the MaRVL Shared Task*
12:30 - 14:00	*Lunch*
14:00 - 15:00	*Invited Talk 3: Lisa Anne Hendricks*
15:00 - 15:45	*Workshop Papers: Archival and Non-Archival*
15:45 - 16:00	*Short Break*
16:00 - 17:00	*Invited Talk 4: Preethi Jyothi*
17:00 - 17:10	*Concluding Remarks*

Language-agnostic Semantic Consistent Text-to-Image Generation

SeongJun Jung[1], **Woo Suk Choi**[1], **Seongho Choi**[1] and **Byoung-Tak Zhang**[1,2]
[1]Seoul National University
[2]AI Institute (AIIS), Seoul National University
{seongjunjung,wschoi,shchoi,btzhang}@bi.snu.ac.kr

Abstract

Recent GAN-based text-to-image generation models have advanced that they can generate photo-realistic images matching semantically with descriptions. However, research on multilingual text-to-image generation has not been carried out yet much. There are two problems when constructing a multilingual text-to-image generation model: 1) language imbalance issue in text-to-image paired datasets and 2) generating images that have the same meaning but are semantically inconsistent with each other in texts expressed in different languages. To this end, we propose a Language-agnostic Semantic Consistent Generative Adversarial Network (LaSC-GAN) for text-to-image generation, which can generate semantically consistent images via language-agnostic text encoder and Siamese mechanism. Experiments on relatively low-resource language text-image datasets show that the model has comparable generation quality as images generated by high-resource language text, and generates semantically consistent images for texts with the same meaning even in different languages.

1 Introduction

In this paper, we consider multilingual text-to-image generation. There are two problems with multilingual text-to-image generation. The first problem is the language imbalance issue in text-to-image datasets. Most text-to-image generation datasets are in English, so it is difficult to construct text-to-image generation models for other languages. Furthermore, since existing multilingual datasets have a small amount of data, a discriminator overfitting may cause problems such as instability of learning in GAN. The second is that generative models have difficulty extracting semantic commonality between languages.This can produce different images for captions with the same semantics but different languages. In Yin et al. (2019), they treat the problem that captions with same meanings in English create semantically different images. We extend this awareness between languages.

To solve those problems, we propose LaSC-GAN for text-to-image generation. LaSC-GAN consists of a language-agnostic text encoder and a hierarchical generator. Language-agnostic text encoder generates text embeddings to be used in the hierarchical generator for the first problem mentioned above. And we exploit the Siamese structure training to capture the semantic consistency between images generated in various languages.

Our main contributions are as follows: 1) By using a language-agnostic text encoder, images for low-resource language text can be generated only by learning the high-resource language. 2) Texts with the same semantics in different languages can generate semantically consistent images using the Siamese mechanism in hierarchical generator to extract semantic consistency between languages. We show the effect of each contribution in experiments using English MS-COCO (COCO-EN), Chinese MS-COCO (COCO-CN) and Korean MS-COCO (COCO-KO) datasets.

2 Related Works

2.1 Generative Adversarial Network (GAN) for Text-to-Image

Text-to-image generation using GAN has advanced a lot since GAN-INT-CLS (Reed et al., 2016). The discovery of hierarchical model architectures (Zhang et al., 2017, 2018; Xu et al., 2018) has produced realistic images that semantically match with texts. However, these models only considered image generation for a single language, and to the best of our knowledge the first paper dealing with multilingual text to image generation is Zhang et al. (2022). The model proposed in Zhang et al. (2022) requires learning for each language. However, our method can generate images from multi-

Proceedings of the Workshop on Multilingual Multimodal Learning, pages 1 - 5

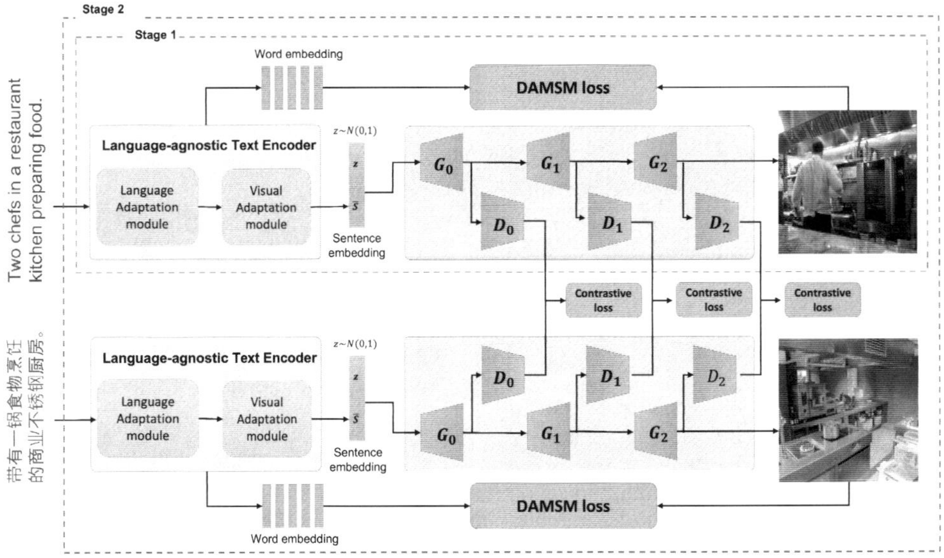

Figure 1: The architecture of LaSC-GAN. In stage1, the model is trained followed by (Xu et al., 2018) with COCO-EN. In stage 2, the text-to-image generation is trained with contrastive loss based on a Siamese structure with COCO-EN, CN, and KO.

lingual texts only by learning about high-resource language.

2.2 Multilingual Text Encoders

Multilingual text embedding models usually use the translation pairs datasets, and sometimes the translation pairs datasets and monolingual datasets are used together. Among these, language-agnostic BERT sentence embedding (LaBSE) (Feng et al., 2020) using MLM(Masked Language Model) pre-training was proposed.

3 Methods

We propose a LaSC-GAN for text-to-image generation. Our goal is to obtain as good visual quality of images created with low-resource language text as images generated with high-resource language text and to enable the model to reflect semantic consistency between languages in image generation. The LaSC-GAN consists of a language-agnostic text encoder and a hierarchical generator. The language-agnostic text encoder is used to obtain a text representation that will be fed as a condition to the generator. The hierarchical generator generates images for text conditions. Training strategy of the model consists of two stages as shown in Figure1. In stage 1, the model is trained followed by (Xu et al., 2018) using only a high-resource language dataset. In stage 2, the model is trained with a Siamese structure with two model branches using data from different language pairs (EN-CN, EN-KO).

3.1 Model Architecture

Language-agnostic Text Encoder consists of a Language Adaptation module and a Visual Adaptation module. We use pre-trained LaBSE (Feng et al., 2020) for the Language Adaptation module and bi-directional LSTM for the Visual Adaptation module. We get language-agnostic token embeddings from each token embedding passed through the Language Adaptation module. Then, the obtained embedding is transferred to a visual representation space through the Visual Adaptation module and used as the text condition of the generator. Hidden states of each token in the bi-directional LSTM of the Visual Adaptation module are used as word embeddings, and the last hidden state is used as sentence embeddings. Our model can use 109 languages used in LaBSE training as inputs.

Hierarchical Generator uses the hierarchical generative adversarial network structure used in (Xu et al., 2018), which consists of 3 sub-generators (G_0, G_1, G_2). Each generator has an independent discriminator (D_0, D_1, D_2). The initial sub-generator generates a low-resolution image by putting the sentence representation $(\bar{s})$ input from the language-agnostic text encoder and a random

Metric	IS ↑			FID ↓			CLIP ↑		
	ST.1	ST.2	ST.1 ∧ ST.2	ST.1	ST.2	ST.1 ∧ ST.2	ST.1	ST.2	ST.1∧ ST.2
EN	14.89	-	-	97.41	-	-	0.227	-	-
KO	12.24	14.76	15.58	103.26	102.04	93.16	0.196	0.198	0.195
CN	14.98	16.14	16.55	97.26	93.64	93.40	0.213	0.214	0.212

Table 1: Quantitative results for each stage of LaSC-GAN. ST, EN, KO, and CN denote stage, English, Korean, and Chinese. ST.1 and ST.2 refer to models that have undergone only Stage 1 and 2 learning processes, respectively. And ST.1 ∧ ST.2 refer to a model using both learning processes together.

noise ($z \sim N(0, 1)$) from normal distribution. The following sub-generators generate a higher resolution image by using the previous generation result.

3.2 Training Strategy

In the first training stage, the model is trained followed by (Xu et al., 2018) using only a high-resource language dataset with DAMSM loss, and the parameters learned in the first stage are used in the second learning stage.

Then, in the second learning stage, we use the Siamese mechanism such as SD-GAN (Yin et al., 2019) to learn semantic commons between texts in different languages. In addition to the DAMSM loss, we compute contrastive loss as follows by using the visual features of the discriminator for the inputs to the two branches of the Siamese structure.

$$L = \frac{1}{2N} \sum_{n=1}^{N} y \cdot d^2 + (1 - y) \max(\epsilon - d, 0)^2 \quad (1)$$

where $d = \|v_1 - v_2\|_2$ is the distance between the visual feature vectors v_1 and v_2 from the two Siamese branches respectively, and y is a flag to mark whether the input descriptions are from the same image or not (i.e., 1 for the same and 0 for different). The hyper-parameter N is the length of the feature vector. The hyper-parameter ϵ is used to balance the distance value when $y = 0$.

4 Experiments

4.1 Datasets

We used MS-COCO (COCO-EN) (Lin et al., 2014) for stage 1. COCO-EN has 80K image train set and 40K image validation set. Each image has 5 English descriptions. We also used the multilingual versions of COCO-EN: COCO-CN and COCO-KO for stage 2. COCO-CN (Li et al., 2019) has 1 manually translated Chinese description for the 18K image train set and 1K image validation set. We used the validation set index of COCO-CN for other languages as well. COCO-KO has Korean machine translation results for all descriptions of in COCO-EN. In stage 2, we use a subset of data from COCO-EN and COCO-KO that overlap with COCO-CN. In stage 2, EN-CN and EN-KO language pair datasets are used for training respectively. The models trained with EN-CN, EN-KO pair datasets are evaluated on the COCO-CN, COCO-KO validation set respectively.

4.2 Implementation Details

The hierarchical generator and discriminator followed (Xu et al., 2018), and the language-agnostic text encoder is comprised of LaBSE (Feng et al., 2020) and bi-directional LSTM. The Siamese mechanism learning method follows (Yin et al., 2019). We freeze the pre-trained parameters of LaBSE when learning the language-agnostic text encoder for stability of learning.

4.3 Metrics

We evaluated the visual quality of generated images using Inception Score (IS) and Fréchet Inception Distance (FID) used by Xu et al. (2018). In addition, we evaluated how much generated images are semantically similar to the conditioned texts through CLIP score used by Wu et al. (2021).

4.4 Zero-shot Language Text-to-image Generation

In this section, we shows the benefits of the language-agnostic text encoder. We trained only on the high-resource language dataset(COCO-EN) in stage 1. Thanks to the language-agnostic text encoder, our model can generate images from zero-shot languages. In Table 1, CN and KO are not used for learning in stage 1 but show metric scores that are not significantly different from EN used for learning. Figure 2 shows images generated in various languages using the stage1 model. The generated images from zero-shot language show similar visual quality to images generated with languages used for learning in Figure 2. In particular, our model can generate images from low-resource languages such as Thai(TH) and Nepali(NE).

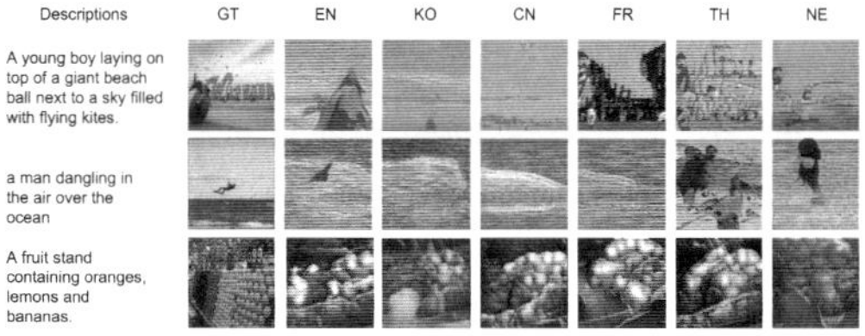

Figure 2: Qualitative results of zero-shot language text to image generation of stage 1. In stage 1, the model was trained using only English texts. GT, EN, KO, CN, FR, TH, and NE denote grond-truth, English, Korean, Chinese, French, Thai, and Nepali respectively. The English description was translated into each language and used for generation.

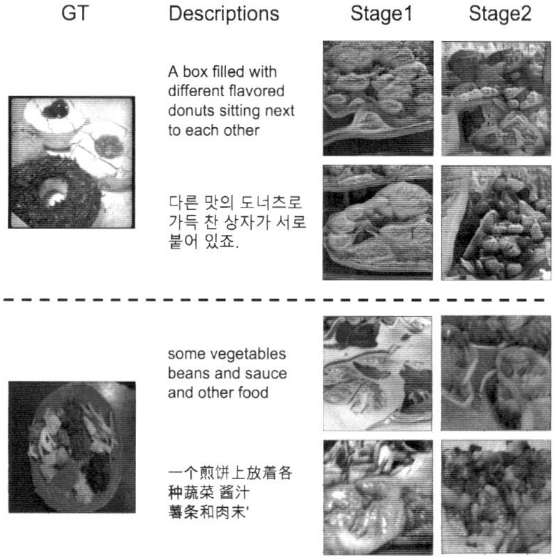

Figure 3: Qualitative examples of the LaSC-GAN. The results of each stage with given a pair of language descriptions

4.5 Multilingual Semantic Consistent Text-to-image Generation

We conducted an experiment to show the effect of the Siamese mechanism training. In table 1, the model that performed stage 1 and stage 2 together showed better performance in IS and FID than the models performed separately. And we compute the FID of the language pairs (EN-KO, EN-CN) to shows that stage 2 helps the model to generate

FID	EN-KO	EN-CN
ST.1	57.74	51.04
ST.1$\wedge$ ST.2	57.32	49.56

Table 2: FID between languages in each stage.

Figure 4: Image generation results of the LaSC-GAN. The images were generated with sentences in which the nouns in the English description were replaced with Chinese and Korean nouns, respectively.

semantically consistent images if the semantics are the same in different languages. As shown in Table 2, it can be confirmed that the distance has gotten closer after stage 2. In addition, images generated from texts in different languages with the same meaning have similar images as shown in Figure 3. And Figure 4 shows the model can extract semantic commons between languages.

5 Conclusion

In this paper, we propose a LaSC-GAN for text-to-image generation. Through language-agnostic text encoder, the model can generate images with low-resource language texts in zero-shot setting. Furthermore, by Siamese mechanism, the model can extract high-level consistent semantics between languages when generating images. The experiments on COCO-EN, KO, and CN show that our proposed method can generate photo-realistic images from the relatively low-resource language text and extract semantic commons between languages for image generation.

Acknowledgements

This work was partly supported by the IITP (2015-0-00310-SW.Star-Lab/20%, 2018-0-00622-RMI/15%, 2019-0-01371- BabyMind/20%, 2021-0-02068-AIHub/15%, 2021-0-01343-GSAI (SNU)/15%) grants, and the CARAI

(UD190031RD/15%) grant funded by the DAPA and ADD.

References

Fangxiaoyu Feng, Yinfei Yang, Daniel Cer, Naveen Arivazhagan, and Wei Wang. 2020. Language-agnostic bert sentence embedding. *arXiv preprint arXiv:2007.01852*.

Xirong Li, Chaoxi Xu, Xiaoxu Wang, Weiyu Lan, Zhengxiong Jia, Gang Yang, and Jieping Xu. 2019. Coco-cn for cross-lingual image tagging, captioning, and retrieval. *IEEE Transactions on Multimedia*, 21(9):2347–2360.

Tsung-Yi Lin, Michael Maire, Serge Belongie, James Hays, Pietro Perona, Deva Ramanan, Piotr Dollár, and C Lawrence Zitnick. 2014. Microsoft coco: Common objects in context. In *European conference on computer vision*, pages 740–755. Springer.

Scott Reed, Zeynep Akata, Xinchen Yan, Lajanugen Logeswaran, Bernt Schiele, and Honglak Lee. 2016. Generative adversarial text to image synthesis. In *International conference on machine learning*, pages 1060–1069. PMLR.

Chenfei Wu, Lun Huang, Qianxi Zhang, Binyang Li, Lei Ji, Fan Yang, Guillermo Sapiro, and Nan Duan. 2021. Godiva: Generating open-domain videos from natural descriptions. *arXiv preprint arXiv:2104.14806*.

Tao Xu, Pengchuan Zhang, Qiuyuan Huang, Han Zhang, Zhe Gan, Xiaolei Huang, and Xiaodong He. 2018. Attngan: Fine-grained text to image generation with attentional generative adversarial networks. In *Proceedings of the IEEE conference on computer vision and pattern recognition*, pages 1316–1324.

Guojun Yin, Bin Liu, Lu Sheng, Nenghai Yu, Xiaogang Wang, and Jing Shao. 2019. Semantics disentangling for text-to-image generation. In *Proceedings of the IEEE/CVF conference on computer vision and pattern recognition*, pages 2327–2336.

Han Zhang, Tao Xu, Hongsheng Li, Shaoting Zhang, Xiaogang Wang, Xiaolei Huang, and Dimitris N Metaxas. 2017. Stackgan: Text to photo-realistic image synthesis with stacked generative adversarial networks. In *Proceedings of the IEEE international conference on computer vision*, pages 5907–5915.

Han Zhang, Tao Xu, Hongsheng Li, Shaoting Zhang, Xiaogang Wang, Xiaolei Huang, and Dimitris N Metaxas. 2018. Stackgan++: Realistic image synthesis with stacked generative adversarial networks. *IEEE transactions on pattern analysis and machine intelligence*, 41(8):1947–1962.

Han Zhang, Suyi Yang, and Hongqing Zhu. 2022. Cje-tig: Zero-shot cross-lingual text-to-image generation by corpora-based joint encoding. *Knowledge-Based Systems*, 239:108006.

Author Index

Association for Computational Linguistics
209 N. Eighth Street
Stroudsburg, Pennsylvania 18360

ISBN 978-1-7138-6747-0

9 781713 867470

CURRAN ASSOCIATES INC.
proceedings.com